MW01245996

The Man Who Thought He Was Jesus

PASTOR GARY M. WASHINGTON

ISBN 978-1-68517-394-4 (paperback)
ISBN 978-1-68517-395-1 (digital)

Christian Faith Publishing
832 Park Avenue
Meadville, PA 16335
www.christianfaithpublishing.com

Printed in the United States of America

CONTENTS

INTRODUCTION

Yes, I'm the man who thought I was Jesus. After years of bondage to fear, demons, and drugs that led to disobedience, evil thinking, bad behavior pattern, and death experiences, for the first time, I had peace in my mind. Jesus stepped in, and I felt like a brand-new person. I had no choice but to believe I was Jesus, as the pastor told me that I was born again and a babe in Christ.

I hung to that belief, crazy as it may sound, and that set me free. In spite of what the psychiatrist and others thought and believed, I held on.

> For as he thinketh in his heart, so is he.
> (Proverbs 23:7 KJV)

I was determined in my mind to hang on to that premise, although I was looking at years locked away in a mental institution. God gave my mother the courage she needed not to sign me away to the plan of the devil, although she did not even know then that she was doing God's will in my life. My mother refused to sign those papers.

My story is written to help change the lives of all who may read it—young and old, rich and poor—and bring hope to praying mothers and fathers all over the world, as a witness, that there is hope in Jesus Christ. He can save you from everything, even yourself that is in cohorts with the devil or evil one. My advice to young people and all is, don't get caught in that trap as I did. If you do, remember, there is hope in Jesus Christ.

Pastor Gary M. Washington

CHAPTER 1

My First Encounter with Demons

It all began when I was about four to five years of age. We lived in a small house in Coconut Grove, Florida, and I remembered everything just as if it were yesterday. And at the time, I was writing this book. I was about three weeks away from being sixty-three years old.

I grew up with one brother named Robert and two sisters, Pamela and Veda. One afternoon, my sister and I were taking a nap. We were between the ages of four and five years old, and I'll never forget this supernatural event even if I want to. It has been etched in my mind. The incident temporarily made me paralyzed with fright and fear. I could not move, because as I looked to my right at my sister, I saw a gorilla, sitting on her back, and I looked behind me and saw a gorilla on my back. The gorillas seemed to be identical, as if they were identical twins.

I tried to warn my sister, but I could not speak. I did not know what was happening to me, but I knew what I saw. And to this day, I can see it in my mind as if it were yesterday. These gorillas were not flesh and blood, and it was as if one could see through them. I did not know that they were evil spirits then and did not know what evil spirits were. I was too young. I did not understand my encounter with these spirits. I later had other experiences, and I told my mother, who told me that I was having a bad dream.

I knew it wasn't a dream, because I was awake and struggling to be free from these gorilla spirits that had attached themselves to me. I would go outside and play and lived like a normal child but was crippled with fear. One of the things I liked to do at that age was to throw rocks at birds and kill them. I could remember that one of the birds we killed, we plucked all the feathers off. If we had the ability to cook, we would have cooked and ate that bird. It looked as if it would have been quite tasty. As I said before, I would play like a normal kid, but when I would go to bed at nights, I was afraid that the gorillas would come back.

CHAPTER 2

Demons Again

My next encounter with demons occurred one night while I was sleeping in the same room with my brother, Robert, who was more than ten years older than me. I woke up and saw an evil spirit that looked like a leprechaun, with a big hat on his head, that was sitting on the chest of my brother, rocking back and forth and looking at me. Now I could see as an adult that it looked like a leprechaun after seeing all the scary movies, but then, all I knew is that it was ugly like an Halloween costume I yelled out a deafening scream that woke up everyone in the house. And my mother came in and asked me what happened, and I told her. Again she thought I was having a nightmare, but I knew it was not a dream. I was awake, and I was so terrified that I could not go back to sleep. She had to sleep in the bed with me that night.

My next encounter with demons was when I was awake playing in the house, and again, I remembered it as if it were yesterday. I walked back into the far room in the house, and I saw another demon that looked like a leprechaun. It was short in statue, and it was sitting on top of the clothes basket. It looked into my eyes, and it knew that I had seen it. It looked surprised that I could see it, and this time, I did not say anything to anyone because I did not think anyone would believe me. The encounters I had with these evil spirits made it difficult for me to sleep at night. I had to be very exhausted and tired in order to go to sleep, so I ended up spending my whole life afraid of the dark and afraid to go to sleep at night. It was nothing but torment that never went away.

To this day, I believed that animals had a spirit in the day Adam was created; after all, the serpent did speak to Eve in the Garden of Eden (Genesis 3:1), and I did see two gorillas—one was on my back, and the other was on my sister. I grew up with two sisters and one brother who were older than I. To this day, I am amazed that I can remember so many things in detail as if it were yesterday. Many cannot remember events that took place at the age of four or even five.

CHAPTER 3

The Move to Richmond Heights

My father was a veteran in the army, and because of this, we were able to move to Richmond Heights which is about fourteen miles south of Coconut Grove in Miami, Florida, to where they were selling homes to veterans at a good price. My mother was a cook at a cafeteria, where we used to live at in Coconut Grove, George W. Carver Elementary School, and we lived right behind that school. My father was an airplane mechanic working for Eastern Airline. But father had to give up the job as an airplane mechanic because he only had a second-grade education, and technology with the airline was increasing. The reason of his second-grade education was he had to quit school and work on the farm helping his mother and family to live.

So with my father not able to work, he joined the organized crime business with the Cubans. My mother continued to work until that illegal business grew, and she became the brain with the bookkeeping.

There were times, even in the first grade, we were left at home alone. I walked four miles to go to school all by myself. I remembered the dark mornings, because I had to leave early. I remembered the dogs chasing me. I was so afraid. Then there was a rumor out of a man they called The Greasy Man, who went around naked stalking people, and this really terrified me.

God protected me even though my father and mother were sinners and did not know God. The scripture said in Romans 5:8, "But God proved his love for us in this while we were still sinners Christ

11

died for us." About the time I was in the third grade, I had sexual lust for the opposite sex. I never saw pornography or pictures of naked women or internet. Back in those days there were no internet. Yet I had these evil thoughts as a child. No one never taught me to do or think evil. It was in my nature to think and to do things evil as a little child. "For I was born a sinner—yes, from the moment my mother conceived me" (Psalm 51:5).

I stole money from my parents. I lied and did other things that I knew were wrong.

This crime business grew, and there were nickels, dimes, pennies, and quarters always lying around the house. As children we thought we were rich, and my mother and father never knew the money was missing because it was so much. We just took it and bought candy from the candy lady store house.

My sister Pam and I would get into violent fights. I would never forget a fight we had to where she bit me, and they thought my arm will become gangrene. We were just in elementary school, first second and third grade, hating each other. I had a hard time sleeping in this house because of very large palmetto bugs. They would make my brother search the rooms and find these bugs and kill them so that I could go to sleep. My brother said, "Why are you afraid? I used to find scorpions in my shoes when we were living back in Coconut Grove."

I remembered in this house the parties my parents used to have, the drinking of alcohol was so bad that they will begin to fight each other. I remembered we used to play, while they were having parties, and we used to see dark little creatures under the tables in different places. And we would say did you see that, and we used to hide under the covers. These creatures were dark and hairy and indescribable.

CHAPTER 4

The House My Father Built

My father's business continued to grow, and he made enough money to build a home, the way he wanted it to be built—custom made. The home was on a corner lot, and he even had enough money to buy the empty lot that was behind it. I would never forget when my father would bring home so much cash that we had to help count the money, and we were just in elementary school. My father said that we were to make sure that the president's faces, paper money, are all lined up together, when stacking the money—twenties with the twenties, tens with the tens, etc.

My dad was one of the richest black men in South Dade, Florida. It wasn't easy to be the son of a rich man because a lot of my friends seemed to envy me, and I got into fights with them. They would ask me how did my father get so rich. I had no answer because I was told to keep things quiet, but people knew about my father's organized crime business. And they kept it *hush-hush*. What happened in Richmond Heights, stayed in Richmond Heights. You didn't find too many people that would snitch because although some may have been jealous of my father, they were proud to see a black man successful, even though it was illegal.

I would never forget when detectives used to watch my father. He used to use me while I was just in elementary school to carry packages through the neighborhood to my grandmother who worked for my father.

My Sister Veda

My sister Veda, whose father was different from my father, was diagnosed as retarded. I believed they use the word *mentally challenged* nowadays. My mother knew something was wrong when she began to wet on herself in elementary school. Veda began to have seizures to where she will pass out and fall on the back of her head. This was horrible to watch. Well, they told them to put a stick in her mouth to keep her from swallowing her tongue. That was something that I don't understand. How could someone swallow their tongue?

The seizures became more violent every day. My sister would run out of the house, and no one could find her. I would never forget the day when it was said that men held my sister in a home and sexually assaulted her, but after my mother's investigation, the men apologized and said that they did not have sex with her. No police was called. In the town of Richmond Heights where I grew up, people usually handle their business privately, without the help of law enforcement. In other words, what happened in Richmond Heights, stayed in Richmond Heights.

So my dad finally had to put a lock on the door from the inside that a key had to be used to open it.

As a result of the incident, my parents decided to put her in a special home for the mentally retarded. My sister became very ill at the age of eighteen, and she died from cancer in her bones. My brother believed that she was overmedicated from prescription drugs that led to cancer, and he blamed my mother for her death. I heard him tell my mother, "You killed Veda."

I remembered desegregation when it began. Desegregation was exciting to me. I liked the idea that I would be going to a school with white children. I love people of all races. The only hate and resentment I knew then was when my grandmother would tell me to stick with my own kind, because I had a crush on a white girl, and she overheard me talking to her on the phone. I would always remember the incident when a white boy asked me to spend the night at his house, and his parents gave the okay. We had to walk a good distance to go to that school, and we had to walk through the woods to get there.

I would never forget the day a white girl and her brother were walking through the woods coming home from the junior high school, and that evil in us caused me and my friends to touch the girl, in places that we shouldn't have, and boy did we get in trouble for that. When the principal of the elementary school found out (he was about six foot three over three hundred lb.), boy did he let us have it? I'll never forget that big paddle and the pain that I felt on my butt, and I was skinny with a small butt. I thought he would break me in half. Back then, they were allowed to paddle, but that law has changed now.

CHAPTER 5

Introduction to Drugs

I learned about illegal drugs in a science class when I was in junior high school. The teacher showed a video of young people getting high smoking marijuana and taking LSD, etc. My friend's older brother gave us marijuana, and we wanted to try because the young people in the video seemed to be having fun. I was so rebellious and a leader of causing trouble. I would never forget the day the teacher slapped me with his hand in my face so hard while we were in class. He did it in front of the entire class. I was so embarrassed. It was all because we were laughing at a movie, and I was laughing the loudest. He knew I was a leader and wanted to make an example of me, and then he had a nerve to tell me to wait after class. He turned the lights off in the classroom, and then it was just he and I alone. I did not know what a demon was, but I felt like this man was evil.

I did not know spiritual warfare, because I was a sinner, but the devil was out to destroy me. I thought this teacher was going to beat me with his hands, and I did not tell my parents because I was afraid. I thought we would have had a lawsuit, but I was too afraid to tell them. I didn't know why, but for some reason, I wanted to sell marijuana joints. I would roll up joints and sell them in school. Someone snitched on me, and I got arrested, when I was in junior high school, for selling marijuana and carrying a weapon which was a knife.

I would never forget that my mother told me I could not go to the prom. They were going to allow me to drive the Grand Prix and have a party at the big beautiful house that so many children never saw the inside. I was so sad and depressed missing that prom, but my mother even though they were doing things illegal, they punished me. And it hurt badly. This caused me to rebel and do evil things. During the following Halloween, me and my friend would hide behind the trees and throw eggs at cars and laugh so hard about it. We would have older people to buy us alcohol to drink, and we would drink and smoke marijuana and do evil things. I was one of the fastest person in the whole school and joined the track-and-field team. They thought keeping me involved in sports would keep me out of trouble. Then I got this bone disease in my knee called *Osgood-Schlatter*. It caused pain in the knee. The doctor told my father that I could be in the wheelchair, or we could put a cast on my leg.

Of course I chose the cast because there is no way I was going to be in a wheelchair.

That cast was from my ankle up to my knee. I forgot how long it stayed on, but it was over a month. My leg was so skinny when they took the cast off. My track-and-field days would be over, but I rehab/recuperated and built that leg back to where it should have been and begin to run track again and do drugs all at the same time.

That bone disease hindered my track-and-field career, but I did recover from it and rehab back to 100 percent.

My mother would always smell my fingers and look for burn marks on my finger to see if I was still doing drugs, but I would use a holder to hold the joints so that she could not see any burn marks on my fingers. She was always checking. She was a good mother and really cared about me. They (my parents) could do things illegal, but they did not want me to do anything illegal. They wanted me to get an education. My uncle, my father, and my mother all really preached education. They preached that more than they did religion. Even though my father, mother, and grandmother did things illegal, my father would buy my mother religious gifts like The Last Supper made out of marble for a Christmas gift.

A lot of sexually immoral things took place in that house when my parents were out of town, for example, sneaking people into the house when they were asleep. My sister and I did a lot of evil things. My father and mother went to the Super Bowl one year to see the

Washington Redskins versus the Miami Dolphins, and we had a Super Bowl party at the house. We did drugs, drank alcohol, and every other crazy things we could think of.

My involvement with drugs continued as I went to high school. I went out with high school white boys whose families were wealthy and were doing drugs. I was introduced to LSD window pane acid, and I would skip school to get high with them. I skipped classes so much until I did not know where my homeroom class was. There were times I got so high until I was blind. One day, around 12:00 noon, I was sitting in my yard. The sun was up, but everything was black. And I could not see for a while. God was merciful to me, the Bible said, "While we were yet sinners Christ died for us" (Romans 5:8).

The sad part about it, I was very athletic. I was one of the fastest in my age group and could have gotten a scholarship if I hadn't got introduced to drugs. When I was in the tenth grade, I ran against seniors who were getting scholarships to go to college to play for Oklahoma Sooners, etc. The drug took its toll on me. I would never forget when the school administrator came out to the track-and-field practice and took me to his office and told me I no longer could be on the team because my grades were too low, and all of this happened because of the drugs and skipping classes, etc. I was able to make straight As, if I wanted to, but I chose the way that was not good—a chosen evil way.

After I was told I was no longer on the track-and-field team, things got even worse. I did more drugs, I skipped class more, chased after girls, etc. My friend and I would break into cars and cut up the peoples' car seats that we thought were teachers. We would set off fire alarms, making the school think that there was a fire, and there was no fire and watch the people leave their classrooms. And we would just laugh hysterically. My father made it worse. He had the nerve to buy me a car. I went to school in that car and sold so much marijuana that I kept in the trunk of the car to sell to the children at school.

A policeman pulled me over, and I thought sure I was going to jail. But I told him that I did not have a key to the trunk of the car he wanted to search, and I talked my way out of that search. That was very scary. Getting into fights and skipping class was the order of the day. The teachers soon had enough of me. One (who was about 6 ft. 6 300 lb.) threw a pen at me because I told him I didn't have anything to write with. He threw it at me, and it hit the floor. And I would not pick it up. He asked me to pick it up. I said, "You threw it on the floor, you pick it up."

He ran into me with his shoulder as he reached down to pick up the pen. Everyone in the class saw this, and then he kicked me out of his class. I went to the office complaining that my shoulder hurt real bad, and to make a long story short, he passed me with a B in his biology class.

Later they told me that teacher got in a car accident, and he died. And even though I was evil, anyone who would try to hurt me seemed to get punished, and it was that way until this present day, if someone tried to hurt me, it seemed like bad things happen to them. And I did not wish for anything bad to happen to them. It just happened. They finally expelled me from class because I would not sit up in my seat. It was a physical education class, and the PE teacher said, "Washington, that's it. Get out of here." That was the last time I went to that high school.

CHAPTER 6

Life at Job Corps

When I got kicked out of school, my mother said, "You are not going to stay here and do nothing. You're going to Job Corps." So I didn't have a choice but to go to Job Corps. I didn't finish the eleventh grade at high school. I went to Job Corps up north where it got so cold, at least for me, because I was born in the sunshine state of Florida. I chose the easiest trade they had—a painter.

Again my mother was so amazing, even though she was the bookkeeper for my father's organized crime business. She wanted me to have a good education and be free from drugs. At Job Corps, I got so homesick. It was unbearable at times I felt like I would vomit. I never knew that I would miss living at home with my family and friends. It took about three months before I got adjusted. There were times I felt under a walnut. I didn't feel like my family wanted me anymore. I felt rejected, confused, and depressed. It was a very difficult time. At Job Corps, because of my depression, I could not focus on my education. I could do the trade of a painter, but I could not focus on getting my high school diploma. At Job Corps you couldn't buy drugs. There were no one selling drugs there, so I had nothing to help me with my depression.

This Job Corps was located in the mountains. It was so beautiful. I remembered swimming in the water that was so clear coming from the mountains. The water was so cold, but you got used to swimming in it. In winter, it got so cold that I thought I would freeze to death. They gave us warm jackets, but that did not help. And then it began to snow, and I saw snow for the first time. The snow was so beautiful. I went outside and played in the snow. I played so hard until I started sweating on the inside, because it wasn't as cold anymore, but yet it was still snowing. Not long after playing outside, I got sick and developed pneumonia. The doctor said I had a type of pneumonia that could last six months. I was so sick. The nurse gave me a shot in my rear end so many times, and she would stick the needle so hard that I thought she was trying to kill me.

I was in a hospital where it seemed all the staff were white even the janitor was white, but none of the employees I saw were black. So in my mind, I was thinking that maybe she didn't like black people. She gave me about seven shots on one side of my rear end. She came in again. I told her, "Please can you change sides? My rear end is so sore. I can't take any more pain." She changed sides and repeatedly jammed that needle into my rear end very hard. I finally told that nurse, "My rear end could not take any more pain. I am not going to let you jam anymore needles." So she went and complained to the doctors, and they gave her a handful of pills, about maybe ten or twelve pills for me to take. I took those pills, and a few hours later, I fainted when I went to the restroom.

When I finally came through and made it to my bed, I was soaked and wet. The fever was a hundred and four degrees, and I was delirious. It seemed as if it was taking to my neck. My neck was on the right side, and my head was on the left side. I would turn to my right and said, "Feel better neck." And I turned to my left and looked at my head and said, "Please get better." My eyes were green and red. I have never been this sick my whole life. I thought for sure I was going to die. By the grace of God, I was out of the hospital in two weeks. A few memorable events took place at Job Corps.

I will never forget when the girls from Atlanta, Georgia Job Corps came to visit us. One of the ladies, who was the chaperone, came to me and sat down and talked with me. She told me that she saw me writing a book. I took a picture with this lady, and I still have it today. I did not know anything about prophecy or prophet because I never went to church, but I guess she was supposed to be prophesying or giving me a word of knowledge or maybe she had a psychic spirit. I do not know. But after forty-three years plus, I am writing my first book.

As we traveled to Atlanta, Georgia, some of the young men at Job Corps would go out and get prostitutes and came back with STDs, but I was not one of them. I was always looking for a girl-friend. Another situation at job Corps that I had to deal with was that the people from up Northern United States, Alabama, North Carolina, etc., did not like young men from Miami, Florida. They called me a *pretty boy*, and they were jealous of me and wanted to beat me to death.

I was 6 ft. 3, 150 lbs., and a man who was six feet 4 in and about 270 lb. wanted to cut my throat. He had the nerve to have a razor blade taped around a toothbrush. He was already bigger than I was and had another young man with him to double-team me. They slapped me in the face many times to provoke me to hit them back so they would have a reason to beat me to death. I could not fight both of them; therefore, I left the dormitory and told the administrator to send me back to Miami. For they threatened my life. I told them that I would not do any work. I would boycott until they send me back. The administrators gave in to my requests and sent me home. Those guys wanted to do me great harm, and they did not even know me. And I was no threat to them. I stayed at Job Corps for eight months. They gave me a certificate and also paid me wages for about six months. But I did not succeed in getting my high school diploma.

CHAPTER 7

Back to Miami

When I got back to Miami, I asked my mother if she was told that the boys wanted to kill me and was she told that I had pneumonia. She said that she knew about the pneumonia. They called her and told her that they would take care of me, but she did not know about the threat of the young men to beat me to death. So my mother said, "You're not going to sit around here and do nothing. Look for a job."

I was blessed to get a job working for Miami-Dade County Parks and Recreation, even though I did not have a high school diploma, but now I wished they would not have hired me because I had no desire to get that diploma after Dade County Parks and Recreation hired me. I felt like I did not need it. I wanted more money, and since the job was part-time, I got a second job, working for Burdines in Dadeland Mall. Now that I was free from Job Corps and working two jobs, I wanted more drugs to feel high, and I began to steal from the company I was working for. I had a friend that was using heroin, and I wanted to try it. I kept wanting to get high. The marijuana just didn't seem like it was good enough anymore, so I used his needle. I did not know that it wasn't good to use someone's needle, and I contacted hepatitis.

I was so sick (from that hepatitis, I gave away my drugs because I couldn't get high anymore). I did not have an appetite. The doctor told me to eat candy and drink milkshakes. My eyes were yellow like a banana peeling. I've never been this sick in all of my life. I thought

I was going to die. I looked at like a zombie. It was a bad experience for me, and I never shot another needle into my veins again after that reaction. I didn't use the needle to get high, but I began to snort it into my nose—cocaine and heroin.

Soon after, I met a young lady and began to live with her. We called it playing house because we weren't married. My parents were now divorced from each other, but they let me stay in that big beautiful house with my sister and brother. So it was easy to impress women to come and live with me. The young lady would do the drugs that I did. It was hard for me to get a good night's sleep most of the time because I was tormented by the gorilla demons. I first saw those demons way back when I was between the ages of four and five years old. Getting high or getting drunk was a good way for me to fall asleep.

(*There is pardon and peace for all, even the vilest of sinner. God is great. He alone can turn a curse into a blessing.*)

CHAPTER 8

Friday the Thirteenth

The first time I ever heard that bad things happen on Friday the thirteenth was while I was working on the park. Everyone was talking about it, and as if they really expected something to happen. It was the last day of our summer program, and we had a party at one of the employee's house. We were drinking alcohol, and for some reason, I made a bet that I would drink a fifth of Canadian whiskey straight out the bottle and still able to drive home. This bet was for money, and I wanted some extra money to buy some drugs. I was so full of the devil, and I didn't care what I was doing. I don't believe any human being can drink that much alcohol and live. I was able to drink all of the alcohol, got into my car, and began to drive home.

The bet was for me to drive all the way home as well, but the last thing that I remembered was drinking the alcohol and that's it. They told me that they took the keys from me and hid them from me, but somehow, I found the keys. And they followed me as I was driving. They told me that I pulled across the intersection, and a van and a station wagon hit me and totally destroyed the car. They got out of their cars and came over and found me in the back seat dead. They said they began to cry out for help. There were no cell phones back then, but a stranger, a white male, who worked at a store nearby, came over and began CPR but could not get a pulse. They said it took about ten to fifteen minutes that I was without a heartbeat or any life.

The paramedics finally arrived and used the defibrillator to bring me back to life. The accident was so bad. Traffic was backed up for hours, and even a newspaper reported it in, there were news the following day. Remember, this was what they told me, because I was in a coma after this accident and didn't remember anything. I woke up in the hospital after this twenty-four-hour coma. The doctor gave me 50-50 chance to live. When I came out of that coma, I began to try to pull the tubes out of my throat because I felt like I couldn't breathe. I thought that they were trying to kill me in the hospital because the tubes were choking and suffocating me. So they tied my hands down, and I began to bang on the bed railing with my ring, making a bell sound. And they came and took my ring off. I began to cry. I thought for sure I was going to die. The ventilators won't work good when you are conscious. They only worked good when you are in a coma. Even though I was a sinner, God was merciful to me.

The word of God said in Romans 5, "But God demonstrated His own love toward us, in that while we were still sinners, Christ died for us."

The doctor said that there was enough alcohol in my body that could have gotten three men pass the limit of being drunk. He believed the reason I didn't have any bones broken was because I did not grip the steering wheel. I was knocked into the back seat of the car. In other words, I was like a bouncing *ball when the cars hit me. I was in the hospital a little over two weeks, and I had to go to the doctor's* office to see him every week because I had irregular heartbeats.

CHAPTER 9

Second Death

The second-death experience came about six months later. My father had a lot of CB antennas that were very tall and powerful with high voltage. He asked me to take down the antenna from one of his homes, and I was smoking marijuana which I shouldn't have been doing because of my irregular heartbeat. As I began to unlatch the antenna and to walk it down, it hit the power lines behind my home. Those power lines were very low in those days. My God, I never felt or could imagine pain that great. Most of the pain I felt was in my chest. I felt my soul been sucked like a vacuum going down a very dark tunnel at a speed I cannot describe. Things that I done in my life was flashing before me like a video. It was like the brain is a computer, human computer, that stored up everything we have done. Matthew 12:36 read, "But I say unto you, that every idle word that men shall speak, they shall give account thereof in the day of judgment." It was like you can't lie on the day of judgment because everything you do is stored up in your brain.

After the paramedics put the defibrillator on me and brought me back to life, I was told by the nurse who lived close to me that her daughter woke her up from her nap and told her that she heard the sound of the electricity and thought that something must have happened to Michael. Most of my neighbors called me Michael which is my middle name.

Just writing this book and telling the story is bringing tears to my eyes, when I think about the mercy of the Lord and Savior Jesus

Christ. When I opened my eyes, my backyard was full with people who witnessed this miracle. Because they did not have cell phones in those days, it took the paramedics over ten minutes to get to the house. I had no heartbeat they said for around fifteen minutes.

The nurse told me after I got out the hospital that I had white foam around my mouth, but she didn't care. She began the CPR, but she could not get a heartbeat. When the paramedics got there, they told her that I've been dead too long, and if they do revive me, quite likely, I would be a vegetable.

Everything that happened to me in my life from the age of four I remembered as if it was yesterday. I could see it so clearly and in such detail and enabled me to write this book of my life story. They gave me my tennis shoes which were burnt with holes in them from where the electricity penetrated my feet. I still have the burn marks on my feet to this day where the electricity exited my body.

When they put me in the ambulance, I could not feel anything in my body. Anyone could have taken a knife and stabbed me, and I would not have felt it. It seemed as if I was empty. I could talk and could not feel. I had no feelings at all in my flesh. I thought I was going to be paralyzed for the rest of my life. I felt like an empty shell. I began to get feelings in my body when they rushed me into the emergency room. The electricity went off at the hospital when they roll me into the emergency room, and I was told they had a power outage all the way from Naples to Key West and in most areas that day.

> MIAMI, May 16 (AP)—A massive power failure cut off electricity to a 15,000 square-mile area of south Florida today, shutting down air conditioning in homes and offices, stranding people in elevators and snarling traffic at busy intersections. (Newspaper article)

The power went out at midmorning and remained out for periods ranging from minutes to hours. The temperature was in the 80s. Power was restored by midafternoon.

The Florida Power and Light Company, the state's largest utility, said that more than a million of its 1.8 million business and household customers were affected.

About 2.5 million live in the area that includes the state's densely populated east coast, from the upper Florida Keys to Miami, Fort Lauderdale, and the Palm Reaches. The outage extended west as far as Naples on the Gulf of Mexico.

Now what seemed to be a coincidence was that I had the same doctor that I had when I had the car accident. That same doctor was assigned to me because he had the same name of my mother's doctor, and even though they made a mistake, he worked on me. When the power went out in that hospital, he made a joke and looked at me and said, "Did you do that? This is strike two with you. I wouldn't go for strike three."

Again I was in the hospital for a little bit over two weeks with irregular heartbeats. I had so many irregular heartbeats. My heart was skipping everywhere. It was not normal. I was told not to smoke and not to drink again, but I was so bound by sin. And I continue to smoke and get high. I used to think I was going to have a heart attack. After I got high, my heart would beat like crazy. I would never forget the day I went in for a visit, and the doctor put a lot of wires on my chest and told me to run up and down. And he kept hitting the machine with his hand as though the machine was broken. I would never forget his words. He said, "I can't believe it. It's like you have a new heart."

The doctor kept telling me not to drink alcohol and do drugs, but I didn't listen. I kept doing drugs and alcohol. I did not have to do anything to be a sinner. I was born a sinner, and it was very hard to live without sin.

Good understanding gives favor: but the
way of transgressors is hard. (Proverbs 13:15)

CHAPTER 10

Another Chance

I went back to work and continued to do drugs and took prescription drugs all at the same time, until my friend gave me a drug that I thought was THC. I would mixed it with the marijuana and would smoke and snort it as much as I could every day. Then one day, I began to think some strange thinking. I began to think that everybody on the job was out to kill me. I didn't want anybody to come near me. They took me to the infirmary on the job, and they called the ambulance to come and pick me up. And they took me to the hospital. One lady on the job was able to calm me down, because I wouldn't let anybody come near me. They did blood work and found out that PCP was in my bloodstream. This was the first time I've heard of that drug.

I lost my job working for Burdines Department Store, but I still kept the job at Parks and Recreation for Dade County. But for some reason, I kept snorting and smoking the PCP. And things went from bad to worse. I thought my girlfriend was working for the FBI, because my father was into organized crime, and I thought she was there getting information so he could be arrested in order to dismantle and close down the crime ring. All these thoughts were not real thoughts. The PCP made me think of things that were not real—only a delusion. These thoughts and actions were results from the devil and a mind in crisis.

The devil must have been having fun because one day I ran out of my house and into my neighbor's house and held her child hostage. I used her as a shield, as I thought the FBI and police were out to kill me. They called the police, and when the police came into that house, I thought for sure they were going to pull out their guns and shoot me. I was getting ready to run through a glass sliding door when they called a friend of mine next door. He came over and calmed me down. I went with the ambulance to the hospital again. The paramedics wanted to put something in my mouth. I guess it was something to calm me down. I told them that if they touched me, I would bite their noses off, so they did not touch me. They tested my blood and found out it was PCP again, and the doctor recommended my mother to take me to the crisis center at Jackson Memorial Hospital in Miami.

My mother, however, decided to watch me to see if I would get better. What I have told you and what I am about to tell you is non-fiction, a true picture of my early life. Some will believe, and some won't. But nothing was exaggerated. Everything was in detail. Some people would ask why did I waited for over forty-one years to write this book. There were so many distractions, not having the resources, etc. The doctors told my mother that someone must watch me at all times, but my mother was busy working. And others in the family had their things to do, so no one could watch me twenty-four hours a day.

One morning, I heard something on the radio about dysfunctional families. I used to sleep with the radio on because it was hard for me to go to sleep without music or a television. That radio talk show made me think it was time to kill my father to get rid of him. I started to look for him in the house. I was going to kill him with my bare hands. I became a kung fu expert in one minute. Thank God, he was nowhere in the house. PCP made me think that he was evil and maybe he was sleeping with my girlfriend, and so many other evil thoughts about him and I had to get rid of him. I ran up and down the house, kicking like I knew kung fu in a rage, when all of a sudden, I sat at the table and began to come to myself and said, "What in the world am I doing?"

I could not believe I wanted to kill my father. I sold drugs for him, and I remembered how he used me as a mule to take packages to my grandmother when police were watching him. And I was just in elementary school. I remembered so much of how he taught me to count and arranged money. My sisters, brother, and I helped count the money because it was too much money for him to count. Everything came back to me about the things he taught me in organized crime. The Cubans, who he used to work for, gave me a large jar full of quarters when I was just in elementary school. I thought I was so rich as a little kid. I wanted to be like my father and the organized crime boss, because of the money. I saw the money and a life full of luxury that my father lived with cars like Cadillacs. He owned grocery stores, nightclubs, duplexes, and so much more, and here I was, wanting to kill him. I sat at that kitchen table feeling terrible that I wanted to kill my father.

CHAPTER 11

Encounter with God the Holy Spirit

I was out of control in every area of my life, when all of a sudden God came into my life and literally touched me. And the electricity power went out in the house, and I heard the power plant that was three blocks away from my home made a loud noise. It was amazing that I did not believe in God, and God touched me. I knew it was God. I cannot explain, but I knew God touch me. And I told my girlfriend, who I was living with, that I was going to church. She said, "You are really tripping. You are going to church! You are really crazy, Gary." I went to the church of a lady, who was a pastor and who came to the hospital to visit me after I died in the car accident on Friday the thirteenth. She was the one I told that the white man wrote the Bible and brainwashed them and that I felt sorry for her and others who believed. Now here I was then, going to her church to get free from this angel dust. I dated her granddaughter years back, and this was how I first met this mother—a pastor of a small church down in Goulds, Florida.

I caught the bus to church because I didn't have a car. It was destroyed in the car accident I had. When I arrived at the church, everyone was at the altar praying, so I went to the altar. And I said, "Jesus" but nothing happened. I said, "Jesus" the second time but nothing happened. Then I cried out with the loudest sound I could make. I screamed his name so loudly, and then I did not know what was taking place. But it felt like a fire, and wind swept through my body and knocked me to the ground. I was on the ground, and I thought to myself that I needed to get up because they knew that I am a drug addict, and they may think that I was overdosed and dying in the church.

And be it strange to me, I was dying spiritually. I wanted to get up because I did not want to embarrass myself and the church. I tried to get up two times, but that wind knocked me back down to the ground. I stayed on the floor at the altar, while everybody went back to their seats, and I remained on the floor. Nobody touched me. They went on with the service. Now I knew what that wind was. It was the Holy Spirit. That fire began to feel good when I yielded to it.

When I finally was able to go back to my seat, I felt like a drunken man. I was very weak, but when I looked outside, the sky was brighter than usual. It was daytime, but things looked brighter. And it began to rain gently, and the rain looked like crystals. Everything looked brand-new. Everything looked brand-new, and I felt brand-new. I did not feel like the same Gary. I knew I was Gary, but I felt like a new human being that never existed before. After church, the mother and her daughter took me out to eat, and I told them that I didn't feel the same. I felt like a new person. I felt so wonderful, and they told me that I was a baby Jesus. That was the term that they use, instead of telling me I was born again. They did not mean any harm, and I did not understand what they were trying to tell me. I felt like a new person, and I did not feel the same. So I thought I was Jesus.

If you are reading this book and when you are dealing with people who are demon-possessed or had a hard life of drug addiction, you must be very careful what you say to them, or best, find someone with past experience in counseling or dealing with drugs, who can minister to them. When I tell people I thought I was Jesus, some people laughed, and some people said I was crazy. But it was a horrible experience for me that brings me to tears at times and even while I'm writing this book. People who never did drugs and never were demon-possessed didn't understand much about the kingdom of darkness.

I am Jesus

So I went home. I was so excited about being Jesus. I told my mother, my sisters, my brother, and my girlfriend. I told everyone I was Jesus, and I was going to save them. I told my girlfriend I was Jesus, and a demon spoke through her and said, "I am Mary, and you got me pregnant." My mother asked, "Where have you been?" I told her about the church I went to, and I went back to that church the following Sunday. And my mother came to the church and picked me up and told me that the church people were crazy, and she took me back to the Jackson Crisis Center for people who have lost their minds.

I went to the Jackson Crisis Center with her to prove to her that I was not crazy. I went to that place to heal all the people who were crazy, because I thought I was Jesus. I told the psychiatrist who had a lot of freckles on his face and blue eyes that he was the blue-eyed devil. They tied me down with scraps. I broke the scraps, and then they chained my legs and chained my hands down. I saw policemen beat people who were demon-possessed or have lost their minds because of drugs. They were beating them in the head with clubs and putting them in straitjackets. This was how they deal with the people who are crazy. They beat them down physically to restrain them.

I might have been crazy, according to the record, but from what I saw, I knew not to challenge them. The psychiatrist had the report that I wanted to kill my father, and I threatened to bite the noses off the paramedics and emergency room doctors. So they did not want to take a chance of me becoming violent. They chained me down like an animal. Again they asked my mother to sign the papers so they could put me away, but again she would not sign.

I was her child, and she would not give up on me. They gave my mother a prescription for me, and I promised her that I would take the drugs. But I did not do it after all. I thought I was Jesus, and I did not need any help. My mother was too busy to watch me twenty-four hours as the psychiatrist instructed her to do. She thought I was taking the medication. I kept the medication as evidence that I

35

was Jesus and that God was healing me. I was exercising my faith and didn't even know it then.

Faith is the substance of things hoped for;
the evidence of things not seen. (Hebrews 11:1)

CHAPTER 12

My Second Encounter with God the Holy Spirit[1]

I called the pastor and told her that nobody wanted to believe that I was Jesus. The pastor was alarmed. She said, "What? You are not Jesus." I told her that she told me I was a baby Jesus. She said, "What! I meant that you were a babe in Christ." I was so disappointed that I wasn't Jesus. I felt like I did not have an identity anymore. I spoke with her daughter, and I told her daughter I found out I wasn't Jesus. And I was so disappointed. Her daughter said, "Well, you know, your name, Michael, is in the Bible." I never read the Bible before, but I looked up the name Michael and found out that he was an archangel. So now I thought I was an archangel.

I wanted to be somebody supernatural because I knew that I wasn't the same Gary anymore. She told me about a revival at Dinner Key Auditorium, where a famous evangelist was going to be, and she told me that I needed to be at that revival. I did not have a car, so I called a taxi. I did not have all the money when I got there to pay the taxi, but the driver said it was okay. So I went to that revival and thought that I couldn't go in as Michael. But needed to go as Jesus because he was the greatest. I was determined to be Jesus. I wanted to go to that revival and blessed that evangelist. To me, he needed me. I walked around that auditorium, thinking I'm Jesus. Over five thousand people were looking at me that night.

I walked right up to the front. The evangelist was speaking, everybody sitting down. I was the only one standing with silk roses in my hand, making crosses to bless that preacher. An usher came and tapped me on the shoulder and said, "Could you please sit down for the sake of the people?" So I went to the back of the auditorium where I saw the pastor's daughter who invited me to that revival meeting. I listened to the sermon, and during the altar call, the evangelist pointed in my direction at the back. And he said, "Either you are a child of God or you are a serpent." I began to shake and tremble. I told the lady that I knew that I was going up to the altar, and she told me to go. I went up shaking, and I climbed up on the platform where the preacher was and said the sinner's prayer.

None of the ushers touched me at this time. I was the only one to climb up to that platform. After I said the sinner's prayer, I saw the fire of God covering the entire auditorium. This fire looked red, but you could see through it almost like an electric heater. Transparent was the only way I can describe what I saw. You could see through this fire. The fire went through my body. I felt like my body was in a very hot oven. I did not know what was happening, but that fire was purging me this time. I did not fall. I was able to stand, but it went through my bones, my mind, my spirit, every part of me. And when I left that evangelistic meeting, I did not believe I was Jesus anymore. I was in my right mind. Glory to God!

About three months later, my mother examined me, and she said, "I'm proud of you that you have been taking your medication."

I said, "No, mama, I saved all the bottles to show you that I did not take one of those pills and that Jesus Christ took out all the angel dust and restored my mind."

My mother did not understand when I told her that Jesus took all of the PCP out of my blood, so she took me back to the psychiatrist. I went with my mother because I knew she did not understand, and I sat down and told the psychiatrist that this will be the last time he will see me. I shook his hand, and I told him Jesus removed all of the angel dust from my blood. And he told my mother that I was worse than I ever was, so she needed to sign the papers and put me away. But my mother looked into my eyes, and she saw that I was perfectly normal. And she said, "I guess you really believe Jesus took away the PCP, and that's a good thing."

CHAPTER 13

The Underworld of Darkness Revealed

> For we do not wrestle against flesh and blood, but against principalities, against powers, against the rulers of [a] the darkness of this age, against spiritual hosts of wickedness in the heavenly places.
>
> —Ephesians 6:12

After I was completely restored in my mind and was made whole physically, Satan and his demons attacked me. The first attack came from a fallen angel, a prince of the air. Fallen angels do not need a body to possess. They could control a person's mind. They could control governments without possessing a body. They had the ability to possess a soul, if they choose to. Remember Judas was a thief before Satan entered his soul.

The Bible said Judas was a thief in John 12:6, "This he said, not that he cared for the poor; but because he was a thief, and had the bag, and bear what was put therein." The Bible said that Satan entered into Judas in Luke 22:3, "Then entered Satan into Judas surnamed Iscariot, being of the number of the twelve." So there was no doubt that Judas was influenced by the power of Satan, but Satan had to enter into him in order for him to betray Christ, because he knew too much about Jesus to do it with his own conscience. Remember how Satan seduced Adam and Eve? He did not have to possess them in order for them to sin against God. Adam and Eve had the intelligence almost like angels, yet Satan outsmarted them. He is a master schemer.

So I was lying in my room asleep when this prince of darkness attacked me. It did not have the shape of a human or the shape of an animal. It had dark swirling eyes like the swirl on a large lollipop. The swirl moved in circles, black and dark. He had control of my body and raised me from my bed, and I asked him what was its name. It gave me the name of a very famous professional wrestler. (I believed now that this prince of darkness was an evil media spirit.)

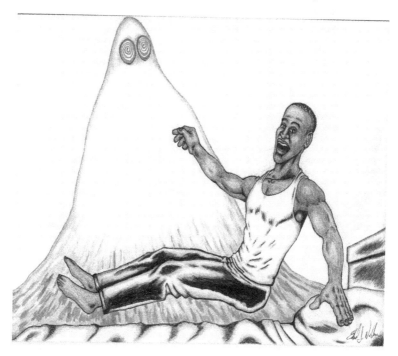

The media is one of the greatest distraction for a Christian. It could break our consecration and sanctification with God. I really believe that. Satan would use the media to brainwash the world. There is no doubt that the movies from Hollywood were designed to destroy the minds of our children. Even some Disney movies were satanic. So as this media prince of darkness was controlling my body, suddenly, I saw the power of God that look like a bolt of lightning that came through my window and destroyed that prince of darkness. Then God put me in a deep sleep. I was able to rest. About a week later, I had a lust spirit jump on top of me. It began to grid on me. I could not see this demon, but I felt him. And in a sexual way, it molested me, and again God sent an angel and made him loose me and took his hands off of me.

I've never seen the angels that helped me. They were so fast. They looked like lightning. God did not permit me to talk to them or see them face-to-face. A few days after that, a demon wrapped me up in the sheets on my bed, until I could not move, but again an angel delivered me. I had trouble sleeping, always afraid that I was going to be attacked. I've had that problem since the age of four, and now it became worse when I gave my heart to Jesus.

CHAPTER 14

More Attacks

The next encounter I had was the gorilla demon that I saw on top of my sister and me, between the ages of four and five. God allowed it to have a conversation with me. It asked to come back into my body. It was amazing because we had just learned in Sunday school the day before that our bodies are the temple of the Lord, and I didn't know anything about the Bible until I began going to Sunday school. I told that gorilla demon that it cannot come back into my body. My body was the temple of God. It had been over forty-one years now. I have not seen that gorilla demon since.

About a week after that incident, as I was sleeping, God took my spirit out of my body. I was at my front door, and a demon with a black band around his head and a bat in his hand drove up to my driveway in an old hearse. It got out of that hearse, walked up to me, toe to toe, face-to-face with such an angry face, that I have never seen before. Its body was red, and he dressed in black. It was not flesh, boy, he was ugly. I did not move to let it know I was not afraid of him. The demon could not touch me. It went back to the hearse very angry and threw an object at me, and God shut the door of my house. I knew it was an out-of-the-body experience. I was like, Wow, demons can drive around in a hearse. He had an assignment to kill me, and he failed. Everything looked like some form of electricity in the kingdom of darkness. That was the best way I can describe it.

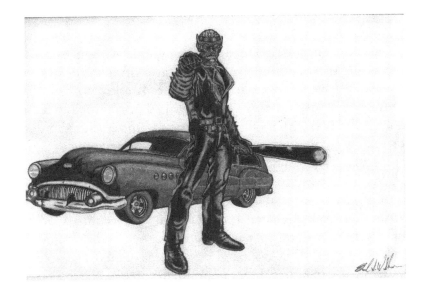

CHAPTER 15

My Visit to Heaven

My visit to heaven came at a time when I was lying in my bed watching television, and in a blink of an eye, I was in heaven sitting in a silver chair. The silver was so pure. You can see through it. It had different types of precious stones around the frame. I looked to my right, and as far as my eyes could see, there were many people sitting in silver chairs. The atmosphere was so pure, clean, and cool. The only way I can try to describe it was like sticking your nose in a freezer of your refrigerator. It was a thousand times fresher than that, and all I could say was, "Wow."

> And hath raised us up together, and made
> us sit together in heavenly places in Christ Jesus.
> (Ephesians 2:6)

In front of me was a pure white cloud, moving in circular motion. Behind the cloud was a loud voice that spoke to me and said, "You got strength now. Go back, go back." God did not let me see Jesus, but when he spoke to me, his voice was like a contained echo. Maybe it was to keep me from being conceited and to keep me humble, because I do talk a lot. It was like a blink of an eye that I left earth, but when I came back into my body, the program on television was gone off. The news was gone off, and The Late Show was gone off.

In those days, the TV just shut down. At least two hours had passed by, but it seemed like I was gone only for a second. It was so real, and to confirm that it was real, I remembered when God said, "Go back. Go back." This let me know that I had left earth and was in the third heavens. If it was up to me, I would I have chosen to remain in heaven. But I needed that visit to heaven, and I needed strength from God because I was under such attacks from so many demons. For God to send me back to earth meant there must be great work for me to do. A few days after that, Jesus came to my bedroom, woke me up, breathe on me, and said, "*Tell them I want to forgive them.*"

His voice was so smooth and so gentle, and so much love and caring was in his voice. This was my mission. This was my calling, and it came from Jesus himself. So I went out into the hedges and highways with such passion, to get people to be saved, and told them that Jesus wants to forgive them of their sins. I even told the witches that Jesus will save them. I remembered when one witch met me at a shopping mall and offered to buy me lunch. I sat down to eat with her because at the time I did not know she was a witch. She was a beautiful witch, so I began to tell her my testimony like I did for everybody else, and then all of the sudden, she put up two fingers to put witchcraft on me. And I put up my hand, and she began to tremble.

She told me to put my hand down. I witnessed to her and asked her how did she become a witch, and she said, "I am not a witch. I'm a hermit." I told her that God told me that she was a witch, and she put the two fingers back up again. I put my hands up, and she began to tremble. She got up and ran from me. When I got home, God showed me a vision of her and others, in a circle working witchcraft against me. I told them if they don't repent, they will all be destroyed, and they disappeared. Witches and warlocks and a voodoo priest have been working against me for over forty-one years, but I thank God for giving me power to rebuke them and to bind them in the name of Jesus.

Behold, I give unto you power to tread on
serpents and scorpions, and over all the power of

the enemy: and nothing shall by any means hurt you. (Luke 10:19)

Also in Isaiah 59:19, "When the enemy comes in, like a flood, the Spirit of God will raise up a standard against them."

CHAPTER 16

Back to the Hood

I would never forget the time I went back to where I used to hang out selling drugs and gambling when I was a teenager. I went a little bit overboard because I was so excited about being free from sin. I wanted everybody to be saved, and I began to shake hands with people I used to hang out with. Some of them began to fall to the ground right in front of all their friends, and they would say, "Man you shocked me." These were men who were drug pushers, drug dealers, gamblers, gangsters, etc.

They felt the power of God, but I was a babe in Christ and did not know how to use the power. And they became afraid of me and ran from me. Even on my job, I went overboard. I didn't recommend that people who will read this book do what I did.

I saw a man walking across the park where I was working, and I called him into the bathroom and began to witness to him. He seemed like a walking zombie. It was amazing to me that this man came into the restroom and allowed me to pray for him. He knew me from working on the park, but to allow me to pray for him was the Holy Spirit at work. He was on drugs so badly. I could see it in his eyes. I took him in that restroom and cast that devil out of him. This man later joined the church I belong to and was the best man at my wedding. He was the first soul I won to Jesus Christ. To make a long story short, this man couldn't read and write very well, but after he gave his heart to Jesus, he got favor from God and got a job working for the government for about thirty-five years. And he is now retired and an associate pastor at a great church.

The pastor at the church I was attending realized that I had the gift of speaking in tongues and knew the Scriptures, as someone who had been saved for a very long time. She asked me to preach, and my first sermon was on Easter. Pertaining to the gift of tongues, I thought it's been misinterpreted.

When the fire of God came into my body like a tornado, I did not speak in tongues immediately. Later I spoke in tongues as the spirit gave me utterance.

> And they were all filled with the Holy Ghost, and began to speak with other tongues, as the Spirit gave them utterance. (Acts 2:4)

So many churches were teaching people to speak in tongues. It cannot be taught. It must be given by the Holy Spirit as a gift. There were others who pray and fast for the gift. The Lord would not withhold any good thing. This is all right. The last thing I wanted to be was a preacher. I was chosen to be a minister for Jesus Christ and chosen by Jesus Christ himself. I have learned sadly that there are so many people calling themselves apostles and prophets, who was not chosen by God. They appointed themselves. Listen to what Jesus said in the book of Revelation, "I know thy works, and thy labor, and thy patience, and how thou canst not bear them which are evil: and thou hast tried them which say they are apostles, and are not, and hast found them Liars" (Revelation 2:2 KJV).

CHAPTER 17

My Wife Sandra

I met my wife to be under a gospel tent. My pastor introduced me to a prophet, a man of God who moved in the gift of prophecy. I had just turned twenty years of age, and he was older than me. The prophet told me that there was a Revival under a tent in Perrine Florida and that if I go, I might meet a young lady there. I went, but the music and preaching were so good. I did not look at the women who was there. I was dancing until I was soaking wet.

As I was getting ready to leave, I looked back, and I saw Sandra who is now my wife. She was eighteen years of age. She was standing alone, waiting for the lady with whom she was living with at that time to take her home. Sandra was so beautiful and dressed so very well. I had never approached anyone this beautiful before I became a Christian or after I was a Christian, so I was very nervous.

I did not know what to say. I felt like I would just start a conversation with my testimony and tell her how God delivered me from great darkness. I tell you, I was very nervous. I gave her my phone number and asked her to call me. She took my number, but she never called. So I thought she was not interested in talking to me. The reason I gave her my number and didn't ask for her number was because she was renting a room with a holy woman of God, and I thought it would be disrespectful to call her at someone else's home.

I went back to that revival. I asked her to call me again. I had to pursue Sandra. I felt in my heart she was right for me, and I didn't even know her. I thought to myself, *If she called me, I know she is the one that I shall marry*. But later after we started dating, she told me she didn't have any interest in calling me. She believed that a man should call the woman. Sandra told me that the woman she lived with said she didn't see any harm with her calling me and I probably just wanted to talk about the Lord. Well, Sandra said if she did not encourage her to call me, she wouldn't have. But I told her if she didn't call, I would have pursued her, anyhow. I'm so happy I pursued Sandra. I could have lost my first love. You might ask why I said my first love. Well, when I was a sinner. I never knew what love was. I felt love from the very first time I looked into her eyes.

Sandra and I was in love with the Lord, and all we talked about was the Lord and the doctrine that we believed. And we had all things in common.

> Whoso findeth a wife findeth a good thing, and obtaineth favour of the Lord. (Proverbs 18:22)

I prayed for a woman who was raised up in the church because I was raised up in organized crime, and I did not know anything about the religious culture. And she had prayed for somebody who have been in the world because she never tasted the world and wanted to be wise as a serpent. Sandra was so pure and so innocent—no night-clubs, no alcohol, and no fornication, just pure and beautiful.

So I continued going to that revival, and they asked my wife to sing one night. And I found out my wife could sing and is one of the best singers in America, in my opinion. I did not know this when I first met her, but when I heard her sing under that gospel tent, it was incredible. People have been saved just from her singing anointing and her holiness lifestyle.

I said holiness lifestyle because as I entered into this holiness culture, I noticed that there are so many people who are professing Christians and have not been born again. And they could sing very well, but they have no anointing from God.

We dated for eleven months and decided to get married on April 5, the same day as her sister's. It was a double wedding—very beautiful and very exciting. We have been married now for forty years as I write this book.

We had a beautiful wedding. It was a double wedding—the first time I've heard of a double wedding. So I was really excited. The church was packed with a lot of people who honor us with their presence. At the reception, there was so much joy dancing and singing, and one of the best guitar players in the world was playing at our reception. After the wedding and the honeymoon, we went back to Miami, Florida, to live in a small town called Perrine. My father had four apartment buildings for rent. My mother told me we could stay in one the apartments as long as we want to, and the rent would never be raised I thought we had it made in the shade.

I was thankful for what my parents did for me, but I just did not want to live in those apartments knowing that they were brought with illegal money. And I was sort of spoil, and I wanted to leave Perrine and move away from Miami to trust God on my own. So I gave up the easy life to walk by faith.

> For in it the righteousness of God is revealed
> from faith to faith; as it is written, "The just shall
> live by faith." (Romans 1:17 NKJV)

So we saw a televangelist on television preaching the gospel in a pretty good-sized church. We felt the leading of God to join that church. I left the churches I was in fellowship with because I wanted to leave the environment that I grew up in. There was no ill feelings about the church I was attending. God was just leading me and my wife to a new adventure in ministry.

I always felt the call to be an evangelist or pastor from the first month I was saved.

Little did my wife know at the time, she was marrying a man with a vision and a mission from God.

We drove an old-used car my mother gave us. It was a Pontiac Grand Prix. It was in bad shape. It had radiator leaks, and I had to carry six gallons of water in the back seat and pull over on I-95 and put water in the radiator when the water will run out. It was kind of embarrassing pulling up the church with smoke coming out the engine Sunday after Sunday, but we love God and made sacrifices with the joy of the Lord in our hearts.

We moved to Fort Lauderdale, Florida, by faith. No job and no money in the bank, but I was promised a job, working for a car dealership who gave me a lie detector test. I failed the test by telling the truth. They asked me did I ever do drugs before. I told them yes when I was a teenager. I did every drug I could find. I lied. I stole. I told them everything. So they did not hire me, but I did tell them that I'm now a born-again Christian. But telling them that I was born again didn't help because they don't have spiritual discernment. I did not have a place to stay. Thank God for a good friend in the church who allowed me to stay with him and his wife. They let us sleep on their bed, and they slept on the floor.

I would never forget before the landlord told my friend he could not have another couple living with him because it's not in the agreement in his rental contract. We were praying in his living room, and he had curtains that you can see through at the window. And he was on his knees saying, "I surrender. I surrender, Lord," and the neighbor saw him with his hands up and heard the cries. And they called the police because she thought we were robbing him. We would never forget the police banging on the door. Thank God, they did not shoot us, and we told him that we were in here praying.

I told the church I was searching for a job and that I did not have a place to stay. Thank God, I did because the people saw me and my wife dancing in church, and we were always smiling and happy like we didn't have a care in the world. The pastor and the people said we did not know, and the pastor took up an offering for me to get an apartment. And that old Grand Prix finally gave up on us, and we sold it for $50. And we did not have a car, but we did have a place to stay. One of the members offered me a job going door-to-door selling old '97 products and Bibles, perfume, colognes, etc. The people would pay like $5 a week without a credit card. He had a lot of clients, and some days I would go home with a pocket full of money. So happy no one rob me because my pockets were full with cash.

But I was thankful for the temporary job, but it did not come with any benefits. So I kept searching every week for a job. I finally found one at a condominium on Fort Lauderdale beach, and they did not do a background check on me which I thought was strange. They hired me right on the spot.

I've never spent any time in jail, but I did some shoplifting when I was in my teens that total it to grand theft. And I was on probation for one year, and my probation officer and the judge said if I didn't get into any trouble after that year, they will sponge my record. That record is still there to this day. But God had given me favor. I became the supervisor of the janitorial department and also did security work for them.

And the side jobs were just a blessing so much prosperity. I worked for one millionaire as a chauffeur for him and his wife about twice a week to the grocery store, to the doctor's office, etc. They pay me thirty bucks an hour and brought me free groceries for three years. Favor after favor with the millionaires, I was making more money than people who went to college.

I told my wife I believe that someone is going to give us a car. She said, "Are you sure?"

I said, "Yes because we don't have the money to buy one." I would never forget one of the men from the church knocked on our door about 10:00 p.m. and said that he could not sleep because God told him to give us a car. It was a Honda Civic, a good car, but he said, "I have to sell it to you for $1 for tax purposes." It was hard to get to sleep that night because of the excitement.

Sandra and I married very young, and we did not use any birth control. And I noticed that we were married for one year, and she did not get pregnant. And I began to think that maybe the PCP and all the other drugs caused me to be sterile and not able to produce children. So the devil just rubbed it in my face, "You can't have any children because of the lifestyle you had. When you were out living in sin, the drugs damage your body."

At first I would listen to the devil and agree with him, but when I read about Abraham and that he was ninety-nine years of age and was getting ready to have his first child, I said to myself, "Well, if he was up in age and had a baby, I know it's possible for me to have one." Now one must remember, this was my first time reading the Bible. I began to praise God in advance for our baby to be born. The second year went by, nothing happened. The third year went by, nothing happened. The fourth year went by, nothing happened, but I did not stagger in my faith. I did not seek any doctors for help. My faith was only in God. We took no medicine or anything. It was all prayer and faith.

I would never forget when my wife said, "Honey, I miss my period. I think I might be pregnant." She went to be tested sometime later, and I would always remember the day when she came to my job in person to give me the good news that she was pregnant. I was overwhelmed with joy and excitement, but then later, the threat of miscarriage was eminent.

And she had to stay home in bed for about four months. We were blessed that two young ladies from the church, we were attending, came and took care of my wife because I had to work. With prayer and those two young girls, my wife was out of the threat of a miscarriage and carried our daughter, Sabrina, for nine months. I would never forget the day my wife went into labor. It was on my birthday, January 29. I thought to myself, *It looks like our firstborn is going to be born on my birthday*. We did not know if it was a girl or boy. We wanted to be surprised. Yes, my firstborn was born on my birthday.

What made it more exciting was that I had the flu on that day. I was very sick, but it did not stop the excitement and the joy that I had. My wife had a normal childbirthing of the baby. I was there and saw it all. I was a little nervous, I must say. I wish I had something to bite on because it felt like I was in pain watching it all from beginning to end.

We waited five years before Michael was born, and I found out from the doctors that I had a condition that could prevent men from having babies. The way I found out I had this condition was while at work one day. I just could not walk. I had to lay down for hours. I went to the emergency room and was misdiagnosed of what I had. When we moved to Broward County, I went to a specialist, and he

PASTOR GARY M. WASHINGTON

told me he might have to do surgery. I said I would like to pray about it. I began to pray, and when I went back to him, he examined me he said, "You don't need any surgery." I wasn't going to allow him to cut me because the area was a very sensitive area.

We prayed about having another child, and Michael was born on January 6. Both of my children were healthy. They did not have any childhood diseases or hepatitis, since I had hepatitis in my blood. Well, that's what they say once you had it, some traces remain. But I believed God removed all of the hepatitis from my blood because they had no disease or trace of hepatitis—nothing from the PCP angel dust, perfectly normal and healthy children. God is good and great. I was healed from the crown of my head to the sole of my feet, and my children were perfectly normal.

CHAPTER 18

Gifts from God

The gift of the word of knowledge and the word of wisdom came upon me mightily, and I would tell people things about themselves that no one knew. God would even give me the names of people I never met and the types of the illness in their body, as I preached and ministered under the power of God. My wife and I were led to Fort Lauderdale, Florida, to join a church where I was a minister for nine years. I felt the calling to be a pastor but did not get the support that I needed to make that transition, so I looked for a church where I could be mentored in making the transition of becoming a pastor. I found one that allowed me to use their bus to go out into the highways and byways to tell the people what Jesus told me, "Tell them I want to forgive them."

Every Saturday, my wife and I would go into the streets with a speaker and microphone and spread the good news that Jesus saves. My wife would sing, and people would come out of their houses in the neighborhoods to hear her sing. I would then preach a short message on how God loves people and share some of my testimony. This was how we started our church (Romans 15:20 NIV).

It has always been my ambition to preach the gospel where Christ was not known so that I would not be building on someone else's foundation.

We also knocked on doors. We did not build a foundation with other church members. These were sinners in the nightclub and in the world living a sinful life every day. Some were demon possessed. I remembered the first demon I cast out, in one of our prayer meetings. The demon was singing religious songs and said that it was his favorite songs. That religious demon was very hard to cast out. It (manifesting through this person) was singing Christian songs and speaking in tongues. It would also say things that I would not repeat and that was so ungodly and vile.

We continued to witness in the city of North Lauderdale, and the city gave us permission to have a parade. We gave out food and clothing and had a picnic at the park. People came from all over the city to be a part of the outreach events that were taking place. It was hard to sleep at night because so many souls were getting touched by God, and we were so excited.

One of our members owned and operated a daycare school and allowed us to use the school to have church, until we were able to save money and get our own building to lease in Tamarac, Florida. People continued to flock to church, and many demons were cast out. And sick bodies were healed. One man confessed that he was healed from AIDS. Many had incurable disease that were healed. And how can I forget the phone call that one of our members had four aneurysms of the brain all in one day.

We rushed to the hospital, and we prayed the prayer of faith that the doctors would be amazed at the healing power of God. Later this woman who was a new member of our church told us she was bleeding from the eyes, nose, and her ears, and she went blind. The woman was healed, and the doctors were amazed. So amazed that they sent her medical records to a university to study why she was normal and well. This miracle caused many to believe and her family to believe in the healing power of Jesus Christ.

The church continued to grow as God blessed us to be on radio and gave television interviews. And of course, we've had our share of trials, as Jesus said we would. The devil has so many ways of getting into people and causing people to cause trouble and division, but this was a part of ministry.

Now is the acceptable time to be saved.

For he says: "In the time of favor I heard
you, and in the day of salvation I helped you.

Behold, now is the time of favor; now is the day of salvation!" (2 Corinthians 6:2)

When Jesus heard this, He said to them, "Those who are healthy have no need of a physician, but [only] those who are sick; I did not come to call the righteous, but sinners [who recognize their sin and humbly seek forgiveness]." (Mark 2:17 AMP)

I had too many testimonies to tell you in this book. This book would be too large and heavy to carry, but as you read this book, keep us in prayer, as I continue to preach for many years to come, God willing.

I have been the pastor at Metro Life Chapel, along with my wife, Sandra Washington, who is the co-pastor, for twenty-six years, along with the MLC leaders.

CHAPTER 19

Family Affair

My Sister Pam

While I was up in Job Corps, I was told my mom made my sister Pam have an abortion. My mom never encouraged my sister to get a job. She always had a place to stay. She was spoil. So as my sister was growing up, she became a drug dealer with the support of my mother and father. My mother even became a mule, transporting drugs in her car. My sister would tell me stories of how she robbed big drug dealers after they got high and passed out, she took tens of thousands of dollars from them. She lived a very dangerous life and had many enemies. I remembered one day she told me, "Gary, you did not see me on the news. Someone broke into the house and robbed me." She told me that when they robbed her, they beat up her drug partner who have $50,000 in the briefcase.

She said, "They beat him up so bad that his eyeball came out of his socket, but he would not let go of that briefcase. The robbers gave a warning shots with their guns which alerted the neighbors, and they call the police. And they left unsuccessful." My sister also told me when she was about nine-month pregnant with her first child, she was robbed, and they put a shotgun to her stomach and drag her through the house. It was the mercy of God that her first child and second child were able to grow up and to function in life because there was so much cocaine in my sister's bloodstream. She would always tell me that her children are miracle babies.

Even as I write this book, my heart is saddened when I think about the terrible lifestyle my sister had. I would never forget the phone call when she called me and told me that she had AIDS, and she couldn't quite understand how she got it because none of the men who she has sex with had AIDS. Then she began to tell me that my brother had AIDS and syphilis all at the same time. They were living in the same house fighting and hating each other continually, and I'll ask her did she bite him when they were fighting because for some reason she likes to bite when she's get into a fight. She was biting me ever since we were in elementary school. She said yes she bit him. A voice spoke through him and said, "Ha ha ha, you bit me." She said it sounded like a voice of a demon.

I said, "That's how you got AIDS. The blood from you biting him got into your bloodstream."

I was living in Fort Lauderdale. My sister was living in Miami, but I would talk to her on the telephone about Jesus. And I would pray for her many times. She would tell me horrible stories on how she would take a bath in the bathtub where water was filling up with blood. At times she could not speak English. Well, I could not understand her. It was a horrible time for her and for me also to endure. Because I love my sister dearly, I finally got her to come to church while we were having a revival. I took her up to the altar to get prayed. She said the sinner's prayer, but she never was healed from AIDS. But she said the sinner's prayer.

She continued to suffer. She was making a change in her lifestyle, but she still continued to struggle.

When I got the call that she had twenty-four hours to live, I went to the hospital to pray for her, and while I was praying and singing Christian songs, she began to clap her hands and began to praise God loudly.

She praised God of clapping her hands so aggressively. I thought the ivy was going to pop out of her arms. I finally told her to calm down a little bit because I did not want them to throw me out of the hospital.

But she said it feels so good, and she couldn't help herself. That was the last time I spent with my sister while she was alive. I got the call the next day that she has passed away.

I wept and cried at the funeral in my mother's arm so much. It was very hard for me to see my sister died at the age of thirty-seven, but God has given me the strength to keep on living and preaching the gospel.

My Brother Robert

My brother Robert was very intelligent. I believed he had one of the highest IQs in Dade County at that time. My brother and I did not have the same father, and it seemed like he was so envious of me because my dad, whose name was Garfield, became very wealthy. And he used to tell me that I will get the inheritance, and he won't. My brother had an evil side about him. He told me he contacted hepatitis from changing my diapers when I was a baby. At times, I thought he hated me, and then there were times when he would come to my rescue from bullies, who were older and bigger than I was and who physically assaulted me.

I will never forget the time when I told my brother about this bully who assaulted me and took off his belt and beat me with it. My brother was so angry. He took me to that bully's house and made that bully put his hand behind his back, and he told me to punch that young man in the face. I was shaking and so afraid to punch, but I did. And then he told me to do it again harder. I was so afraid of that young man because he had a mental disorder, and I thought he would retaliate.

My brother, Robert, whom we call Bobby, loved to listen to music from artist Black Sabbath, Alice Cooper, Jimi Hendrix, and Led Zeppelin, and he would turn the music up very loudly. Because my brother was older than me, I emulated him and did whatever he did. I followed his ways, and I began to love the music that he listened to. Some of the words in one of the songs went like this: Children of the world today are children of the grave, living just for dying and dying just to live. Some of the words were too graphic. I won't even mention. Now I knew it was Devil worship music that brainwashed my soul.

To this day, I didn't know why my brother liked the Swastika symbol. He drew it all the time. I knew that he had mixed ancestry—*White* because of his father. Bobby's IQ was very high, and he wanted everyone to know it because he liked to belittle others all the time. So even though my brother envied me because he may have thought that I would inherit all the money from my father's business, my father gave him a job, working at his grocery store. I believe the grocery store was a front to cover up the illegal money that he, my father, was making.

At one time, my father owned a nightclub and many duplexes that he rented out. My dad helped my brother to buy his first car, which was a Road Runner, and boy did he drive that car fast. I was afraid to ride in the car with him. He would take off so fast that it made my head stuck to the upper seat.

Many nights he would come home and run in the house after he hid the car behind trees or someone's house because the police was chasing him. You could hear the sirens all over the neighborhood, but they never caught him. And he thought that was exciting. He used to laugh so loudly on how he got away, and the danger of how he almost got killed in an accident. *Pretty boy player* because of his mixed blood, his hair was curly and slick, and women loved the red men back in those days. My brother had so many women that he had a book with the names of the women he dated. He would put a star by the name of everyone he had sex with. It was like a sports competition, but my brother was the only player. And I wanted to be just like him.

My brother moved to Miami—the worst part of Miami. He grew dreads and told me he was the first American Rasta. As he got worse with this disease, he would call me and make clicking sound with a 357 gun that he had and told me he was going to drive by my home and shoot up everybody. That AIDS made my brother more crazy. He had already killed a man with that 357 when he was a taxi cab driver, and the police said it was self-defense, because the man was robbing him. In the final weeks of my brother with AIDS who was dying, he began to spill his guts and tell me just about everything how he was raped by relatives in whom I won't mention when he was just a boy, but he said he would not let them touch me. He protected me.

When we finally got the call that he was dying, won't be alive within twelve hours, I went to the hospital, and amazingly my brother was paralyzed. He could not open his mouth to speak, so he had no choice but to listen to me. I told him about hell. I told him I was on my way there when I had that accident, shocked by that CB antenna hitting the power lines and saw my soul in that dark tunnel. And I accepted the gift of salvation to deliver me from hell, and he could do the same.

I said to him, "Bobby, you don't want to go to hell." He could not talk, but he looked at me in my eyes. And I told him that he had to accept Jesus Christ on his deathbed, if he wanted him to save him from his sins. I asked him to try to move one finger if he wanted to receive Jesus as his savior. He did with all his might to move that finger. My paralyzed brother moved his finger, and I told him to repeat the sinner's prayer in his heart and that he did not have to open his mouth.

I hoped to God that my brother made it to heaven because a deathbed repentance is like playing Russian roulette.

Mother, My Beloved

After my sister Pam died, I knew it was impossible for my mother to raise her grandchildren because she was a diabetic, and her illness did not give her quality time to raise her grandchildren. So my wife, Sandra, and I prayed about moving them in with us, which was a difficult decision, because none of them knew the Lord Jesus as Savior. And I would be making a sacrifice moving them into a Christian home. So we prayed about it, and we decided to move her and my niece and nephew in, and my mother had a quick temper before she received Jesus as her savior. Her illness made her more fussy. But I moved them in by faith, because of the love I had for my family. Even though she was not a Christian, my love for her made me decide to make the move. When she came to us, she was taking insulin shots in her stomach for the diabetes. So I prayed to God and asked him to give my mother the gift of salvation. The Holy Spirit taught me to pray for her to be healed of the diabetes.

I always had faith for praying for sick people. I used to feel fire in my hand, and oil used to come out of my hand when I pray for people. So I prayed the prayer of faith over my mother, and when she went to the doctor, he took her off the insulin. My mother was amazed, and this was the first step in getting her to give her heart to Jesus. I remembered when I gave the altar call at church, my mom came up. The power of God was on her, so mightily she began to shake weep and cry before the Lord; she said the sinner's prayer and gave her heart to Jesus. When we got home, my mom said it is so wonderful to be in church, and she said I wish I had done this a long time ago. As I preached my sermons, mom would write and take notes. She was so hungry for more information about the Lord. After the Lord took her home to heaven, I saw the notes in her notebook, and wow she did load up a lot of information: she was very intelligent. I miss my mother. She will always be in my heart forever.

My father was very stubborn. It took so many heart failures, strokes, and diabetes in order for God to get his attention. My dad was amazed after hearing me preach and living the life of holiness. He would cry many times in church after hearing me testify, because he knew that I came from a very dark place. After all, I was his son, and his Satanic roots were very rooted in me. My father never was physically healed, but he lived about two years more than what the doctor had expected him to live.

His spiritual soul was healed, and salvation was completed in him. He wanted to come to church, so he would take the oxygen tank with him. But he could hardly sit up on the wheelchair, but he wanted to come so badly.

CONCLUSION

It was about seventeen years after I became a pastor that my father called and wished me a Merry Christmas. I lost contact with him. I did not know where he lived. But he finally contacted me and asked me to come to Lake City, Florida, and take him out of the veteran nursing home and could I buy him a trailer in Fort Lauderdale near me and that he would have a friend to come and be a companion to him while he was sick. I agreed to his wishes even though he never call for seventeen years to see how I was doing or to say hi to his grandchildren. The love of God in me caused me to forgive and to love my father. I would never forget when I went to that veteran nursing home to sign him out. The nurses said, "Your father may not make it to Fort Lauderdale. He is very sick." I signed the papers and told them if he dies in my car on the way to Fort Lauderdale, I must honor his wishes. He do not wish to die here at this nursing home. With prayer, have faith. My father live for almost two years after he left the veteran nursing home. Both he and my mother would not come to the church for seventeen years, but I prayed for them every day.

Now is the acceptable time to be saved.

> For He says: "In the time of favor I heard you, and in the day of salvation I helped you. Behold, now is the time of favor; now is the day of salvation! I come not to call the righteous." (Berean Study Bible 2 Corinthians 6:2)

> When Jesus heard this, He said to them, "Those who are healthy have no need of a phy-

sician, but [only] those who are sick; I did not
come to call the righteous, but sinners [who recognize their sin and humbly seek forgiveness]."
(Mark 2:17 AMP)

It was just amazing how my mother and father, who were
divorced for about twenty years, ended up becoming members at our
church, and I was the baby in the family.

Satan's assignment was to destroy everybody in my family. My
two sisters died on the date the thirteenth, and I almost died on
Friday the thirteenth that would have been three people dying on
the day date of the thirteenth. My grandmother died on Halloween.
My brother died on 9/11. My mother who loves information died
on 4/11.

But look at God, my daughter was born on my birthday, and
my granddaughter was born on my mother's birthday.

In my conclusion, I must confess to you that I was stricken with
COVID-19. I thought I would never get it. I was standing on the
word of God.

There shall no evil befall thee, neither shall
any plague come nigh thy dwelling. (Psalm
91:10)

But I understood I had to rightly divide the word of God and
have a balance in my spiritual life, so I stood on this scripture:

Many are the afflictions of the righteous:
but the Lord delivereth him out of them all.
(Psalm 34:19)

Nothing like this has ever happened to me since I've became a
born-again believer in Christ Jesus. I had coronavirus pneumonia,
and I felt like I was going to die. So I prayed that God would take my
life. I said I've been a Christian for forty-two years. I've been married
for over forty years. I fought a good fight, and I said it in front of

my wife. And she cried and told me, "Do not say that. I don't want to lose you." But I told her there's no need for me to live. I couldn't breathe. We have stairs in our home, I could not climb three steps without running out of breath, so I just fell to my knees on the stairs and cried. I was so helpless. My wife could not carry me up the stairs at 198 lb., so I took my time and crawled up the stairs.

I told my wife that she must call 911 because I don't think I'm going to make it. I never been this helpless ever in forty-two years since I've been a minister and a servant for Christ. I must say this was the biggest mountain I ever had after being a born-again believer.

The paramedics came to my home, and as they were taking me away, my wife cried at the door, "Please come back to me, Gary. Please come back home to me. Don't leave me."

When she said that I said to myself I cannot leave her, I cannot leave my wife like this. I grabbed a hold of faith that I didn't know I had.

I said within myself, "I don't understand why, but I have to fight to live. I can beat this with prayer and medicine."

The paramedics said, "Good news. Your vital signs look okay." And when I got to the hospital, I had a hundred and 3.9 temperature.

They couldn't understand how I was breathing on my own at 95 percent, and they told me that they are studying me aggressively.

I didn't know how I was breathing at 95 percent either, but every time I cough, it felt like I was suffocating. And I would continue to cough for a long time, so it was tormenting.

The man that was in the hospital room with me cough so badly. It felt like an avalanche of coughing, and every time he cough, I will cry and pray for him.

This man had to have oxygen to help him breathe. I did not need any oxygen, so he was worse off than I was.

This patient was in the same room as I was, and he began to cry and cry so much. I told him don't give up, and he said, "I'm not afraid to die. I am ready to die, but I have a wife at home and two teenagers."

I said, "Sir, you are not going to die, and it is a blessing that you are coughing because if you are not coughing that means they will put you on ventilation in ICU."

I told him that God made our body to cough when there is something inside of us that don't belong. Because I tell you, I have never heard anyone cough this loud and this bad in my whole life.

So he told me, "I never thought of it like that."

I said, "Yes, sir, your organs are working, and you are coughing."

I prayed for him, and I prayed for myself. We had prayer every day, and we praised the nurses for being warriors who are taking care of us.

I began to tell him that I was a pastor, and he said, "Wow God sent you to me because I was ready to die, but you are my angel. I was ready to give up. I lost all hope."

We did lose our appetite, but on the second day, I began to eat even though I could not taste the food. I ate anyway because I needed all the nutrition that I could receive.

Then the heart doctor came in and told me they found my heart had irregular heartbeats.

So she asked me did I have any heart trouble or did I have any heart trouble in the past. I told her I had cardiac arrest about forty-three years ago in a car accident and six months later the CB antenna hit the power lines, and I was electrocuted died and had an irregular heartbeat from both accidents.

But I told her my heart was in good shape. The heart doctor forty-three years ago was amazed. He was so amazed that he didn't charge me anything and told me to get out of his office and that I had a new heart.

So I told her, "I believe the COVID-19 put a strain on my heart because of a lack of oxygen and wearing the mask."

I also told her I am not a doctor, but I have a strong good heart. So she insisted to give me an ultrasound.

She came back the next day and said, "We found nothing with the ultrasound, but I'm going to keep you on blood thinners just in case. I don't want you to have a stroke."

About the fourth day, my appetite began to come back, and they told me on the fifth day the antiviral medicine that they were giving me would remove the coronavirus.

So they told me to walk up and down on the fifth day. They wanted to test and see how my breathing was. It went from 95 percent to 97 percent. They said, "Well, we're going to release you tomorrow."

I'm not telling anyone to do what I did. but when I got home, I could not continue to take the blood thinners. They made me very weak.

So I stopped taking the blood thinners, and on the second day, I began to get stronger walking up and down in my house.

Went to see my primary doctor, she gave me a good bill of health and released me to go back to work. I believe in prayer and medicine. I am not against doctors, but I always try God first.

I have too many testimonies to tell you in this book. This book will be too large and heavy to carry, but as you read this book, keep me in prayer, as I continue to preach for many years to come, God willing.

I have been a pastor at Metro Life Chapel, along with my wife, Sandra Washington, who is the co-pastor, for twenty-seven years along with the MLC leaders.

Because of the abuse of drugs when I was a teenager, I had some memory loss, but through prayer and my wife encouraging me to finish high school at the age of sixty, I was inspired to write this book of my life story. Sandra, my wife, is truly a help meet, and it was kind of ironic that her name means *helper of mankind*.

A lot is going on in the year of 2020. In spite of the pandemic, the blessings of God have come upon my life in a mighty way. My daughter, Sabrina, was engaged to be married this year to James Jenkins. Can't wait to walk her down that aisle. My son and his girlfriend, Nyla, had our first grandbaby—beautiful baby Sandra, who was named after my wife, and the doctor who helped with the birthing was also named Sandra. Baby Sandra was born on my mother's birthday, and my daughter was born on my birthday. Only God can do these things. I had the honor to marry my son and his girlfriend

71

with a bonus grandson named Max—Nyla's firstborn. Everything by God was and is planned. The Bible said, "In the heaven he rules all."

Pastors Gary and Sandra Washington
Metro Life Chapel
P.O. Box 771573
Coral Springs FL 33077

ACKNOWLEDGMENTS

I would like to thank my wife, Sandra, as we celebrate forty years of marriage on April 5, 1980. It seemed so fitting to write this book during our wedding anniversary.

I would like to thank the following persons as well:

Everyone at Metro Life Chapel—my spiritual children have prayed for me and lifted me up when I was down and have supported the vision that God has given me.

I'm not the smartest person in the world when it comes to writing a book, but through God's leading, I have two persons who have helped me:

Dr. Cynthia Smith-Hughes, an outstanding teacher.

Mr. Rick Olson have supported me behind the scenes and played a great part in getting this book out to the public.

Thank you to all my social media friends and relatives. I felt your prayers and your love.

It is my prayer that this book will bring salvation, hope, help, and life to a dying world. May everyone who reads it pass it on to help others find life in and through Jesus Christ, our Lord.

Pastor Gary M. Washington
Metro Life Chapel
Lauderhill, Florida
USA

ADDITIONAL READINGS

> Having a form of Godliness, but denying the power thereof: from this turn away. (2 Timothy 3:5)

During my twenty-seventh year as pastor of Metro Life Chapel, I noticed that there are thousands of people who call themselves Christians but do not live the holy life instructed in the word of God. *I found this disturbing.*

> This people draw nigh unto me with their mouth, and honor me with their lips; but their heart is far from me. (Matthew 15:8)

The hardest demons I ever had to cast out was a religious demon. The evil spirit would sing Christian songs and speak in tongues, and when the Holy Spirit gave me discernment and I called them out, they would scream with such a loud voice that will hurt your eardrums.

> I know thy works, and thy labor, and thy patience, and how thou canst not bear them which are evil: and thou hast tried them which say they are apostles, and are not, and hast found them liars. (Revelation 2:2)

I have seen so many people that call themselves apostles and prophets but are not. There were so many lives have been destroyed because of false prophecies, so many marriages that ended up in divorce, and so many churches were divided up because people think they are called to be pastors, but they were not.

> For if a man thinks himself to be some-
> thing, when he is nothing, he deceive himself.
> (Galatians 6:3)

I heard people say God said so many times, but they have not won one soul to Jesus in twenty years. These were sad events that are taking place in the last days. My assignment was to preach the truth and root out the stronghold and familiar spirits that have plagued the body of Christ. Under the ministry that God has given me, many have received the anointing that destroy the yoke of denomination and have been set free.

I would never forget the time when oil would come out of my hand with gold sparkles, and so many wanted me to lay hands on them to be healed. There were times when I would shake a sinner's hands, and they would ask me, "Why did you shock me? What was that I felt?"

I prayed to God, "God, can you hold back the anointing just a little bit so I won't chase the sinners away." My first book came at a time during the pandemic, but God has sustained our church. Everything that can be shaken would be shaken.

> And this word, yet once more, significant
> the removing of those things that are shaken, as
> of things that are made, that those things which
> cannot be shaken may remain. (Hebrews 12:27)

Many have stopped giving because they're not attending the church building, but there were a *faithful few* who are helping the church in a tremendous way.

> Now the Spirit speak expressly, that in the
> latter times some shall depart from the faith,

giving heed to seducing spirits, and doctrines of devils. (1 Timothy 4:1)

So many have said we don't have to go to church in order to serve God, and all the preachers want was your money. These were doctrines of the devil to lead people away from the spirit of leadership that have been ordained by God according to the Bible.

And he gave some as apostles, and some as prophets, and some as evangelists, and some as pastors and teachers, for the equipping of the saints for the work of service, to the building up of the body of Christ. (Ephesians 4: 11–12)

Because of Covid-19, most of our ministry has been on social media, and so many people who have never been to our church from all over the world were testifying how God has blessed them through the preaching of the word. I did not have to see the person or touch the person. I could send the word, and the anointing will heal.

RECOMMENDATIONS

A book worth reading; an author worth knowing.

I have known the author, Pastor Gary M. Washington, for about twenty years, and he was truly blessed of the Lord, anointed by the Lord—one who has stayed true to his calling, without compromising.

His story epitomized God's love for us all and would remind the reader that God can truly do all things (Jeremiah 32:27). He is a walking, talking miracle, and he wanted to share his experiences with you, with the hope of leading others to a great and mighty God, the great physician, and spread the good news of the kingdom. God's wish is for all to know of his grace and enter here on earth and in the hereafter—everlasting life.

After reading this book, with an open mind, you will never be the same. May God's richest blessings be yours.

Cynthia Smith Hughes, Ed. D

I want to thank God for the supporters of this book:

Raymond Blackwood
Sheila Browne
Rajendra Persad
Jennifer Persad
Geraldine Cooper
Margaret Blackwood
Meggon Bailey

Linda Frederick
Minnie Goodwin
Bernice Harris
Michael Washington
Nyla Washington
Sabrina Jenkins
Maureen Johns
Mavis McAnuff
Handle Miller
Diana Morgan
Lamont Morgan
Richard Olson
Adrianne Maitland
Deanna Stinson
Venus Stinson
Vernell Thomas
Sampson Williams
Tomeka Williams

ABOUT THE AUTHOR

I'm Pastor Gary M. Washington, a man who did not believe there was a God. I grew up in Miami, Florida, with a family who was control by evil spirit. In my autobiography, you will find out how God got my attention and how I was transformed from darkness into the light. And because I saw the light, I've have nothing but love for all those who don't know God. I have shared my testimony on some of the most leading Christian television and radio network in the world. And since my testimony was so long, I never was able to share it in its entirety.

Christian Faith Publishing Company has given me an open door to share my story to the masses to where I am humbly thankful. Because I did not believe in God, God himself had to reveal himself to me. I had no intentions on being a preacher because I thought all preachers were brainwashed and hypocrites. But now I have been preaching over forty-two years and pastoring Metro Life Chapel for twenty-seven years along with my wife and co-pastor, Sandra Washington. Sandra and I were blessed with our first child, Sabrina, who was a miracle from God and my son, Michael, whom God allowed us to plan having him as our second and only the children we have. I was chosen by God to preach his word so many people have been set free from drug addiction and even self-righteousness because of the supernatural deliverance I receive from the Holy Spirit.

Printed in the USA
CPSIA information can be obtained
at www.ICGtesting.com
CBHW070843031024
15215CB00094B/3276

9 781685 173944